MOVING

BEYOND

FAILURE

LESSONS FROM THE LIFE OF PETER

MOVING
BEYOND
FAILURE

LESSONS FROM THE LIFE OF PETER

BILL CROWDER

DISCOVERY HOUSE
PUBLISHERS®

Feeding the Soul with the Word of God

P.O. BOX 3566, GRAND RAPIDS, MI 49501-3566

Requests for permission to quote from this book
should be directed to:
Permissions Department
Discovery House Publishers
P.O. Box 3566
Grand Rapids, MI 49501
or contact us by e-mail at permissionsdept@dhp.org

Cover design by Stan Myers
Cover photo by VistaKWH via Getty Images
Interior design by Steve Gier

ISBN: 978-1-57293-724-6

Printed in the United States of America

Printed in 2012

CONTENTS

INTRODUCTION

EARTHQUAKES MOVE ROCKS—and people. And when the ground under our feet begins to shake, our view of the world changes.

Something like that happened to a first-century fisherman named Simon. When Jesus came into his life, the ground under his feet began to shake.

In the following pages, RBC Associate Bible Teacher Bill Crowder gives us a fresh look at a series of unexpected events in Simon's life that shook him to the core but that Jesus used to transform him into Peter, which means "rock."

There's a lot that we can learn from Peter's struggle to become "rocklike"—stable and consistent. And in the strength that only Jesus can give, we too can have victory over our failures.

—MART DeHAAN
RBC MINISTRIES

WHEN THE
EARTH MOVES

I N THE MID-1980S, my wife and I moved our
little family to Los Angeles so I could pastor
a church there. Within months of our arrival
on the West Coast, we found ourselves smack in
the middle of the Whittier earthquake of 1987.

Where do you hide when the ground itself
shakes? Where do you run for cover when terra
firma is no longer firm? It was one of the most
unsettling experiences of my life.

Earthquakes come suddenly and without
warning. And they are a picture of the kind of

instability that can shake our lives. In addition, they force us to admit that we are frail and inadequate. They force us to see things about ourselves that we probably would rather not know.

Having experienced an earthquake and its resulting emotional impact, I'm reminded of a man in the Bible whose life was profoundly affected by a series of unexpected moments and events that shook him to the core. His name was Simon, son of Jonah—who later became known as Peter.

Peter's story can be told around some of the earthquake-like moments that shook him out of self-confidence and deep conviction and into emotional episodes of fear and indecision. As a result, we can view his life by comparing it to a seismic graph that shows times of relative stability marked by occasional quakes and tremors that helped to define his life and bring him into a deeper awareness of his spiritual need.

THE MAN AND
THE MESSIAH

P ETER'S SPIRITUAL JOURNEY began, or at
least changed dramatically, when he
was introduced to the long-awaited
Messiah of Israel.

John the Baptist had been preaching his
message of repentance and had gathered a
number of followers. But then he began to
turn their focus away from himself to Jesus
of Nazareth. He wanted to make it clear that
Jesus, not himself, was the promised Messiah
of Israel. One of John's followers, a Galilean

fisherman by the name of Andrew, turned
from John the Baptist to follow Jesus and then
brought his brother Simon to meet the teacher
he believed to be the Messiah.

*One of the two who heard John speak, and
followed Him, was Andrew, Simon Peter's
brother. He first found his own brother Simon,
and said to him, "We have found the Messiah"
(which is translated, the Christ). And he
brought him to Jesus. Now when Jesus looked at
him, He said, "You are Simon the son of Jonah.
You shall be called Cephas" (John 1:40–42).*

Cephas is Aramaic for the Greek name
Petros, which literally means "stone" or "rock."
In that announcement, Jesus did more than give
Simon a nickname. He changed his name in
anticipation of what He would do with Peter.

A stone or a rock is a picture of stability. But
the name that Jesus gave Simon seems to conflict not only with his personality but also with
some of the events of Peter's life over the next

three years. In comparing Peter to fireworks, one writer said that Peter was not like a sparkler or a smoke bomb—he was like a rocket with a faulty fuse. He was too rough, too outspoken, and too underqualified.

Nevertheless, Jesus called him. Simon was not a man who would be quietly tucked in on the fringes of Jesus' followers. He was high maintenance. Though unpolished, untrained, and uneducated, he would become the spokesman of a group that would turn the world upside down.

Still, Peter may be the easiest disciple for us to relate to. The Scriptures make his life an open book by describing not only his strengths and successes but also his unexpected failures that rocked him to the core.

Let's look at four of these defining moments in the next four chapters.

15

SHAKEN BY THE POWER OF CHRIST

I N LUKE 5 WE FIND Peter so shaken by his encounter with Jesus that it led to a seismic shift in his thinking.

A CALL FOR PETER'S INVOLVEMENT

So it was, as the multitude pressed about Him to hear the word of God, that He stood by the Lake of Gennesaret, and saw two boats standing by the lake; but the fishermen had gone from them and were washing their nets.

Then He got into one of the boats, which was Simon's, and asked him to put out a little from the land. And He sat down and taught the multitudes from the boat (Luke 5:1–3).

The scene is the "Lake of Gennesaret" (the Sea of Galilee). The crowds were gathering to hear Jesus teach, and a small group of fishermen were also there cleaning their nets after a long night of fishing.

Today, most of us think of fishing as something to do for relaxation and sport, but for many men in first-century Galilee, fishing was about survival. It taxed every ounce of their energy as they rowed, cast nets, and hauled in the nets. On this occasion, the boats and nets had been empty all night. In that setting, Jesus focused on one of the boats and its owner—Simon.

As we've already seen, this was not the Teacher's first contact with Peter (Matthew 4:18–20; Mark 1:16–20; John 1:40–42). Prior to this, Peter had become a nominal follower of

Jesus. But now the Messiah was laying claim on all that Peter was—and He began by using what little skills and abilities Peter appeared to have.

Jesus sat down to teach, using Simon's boat as a pulpit—and for Simon, what was about to happen would so shake his world that Luke would later record, "When Simon Peter saw it, he fell down at Jesus' knees, saying, 'Depart from me, for I am a sinful man, O Lord!' " (Luke 5:8).

What was it that would bring Peter to this point? The events leading up to that moment deserve our thoughtful attention.

AN INDICATION OF JESUS' IDENTITY

When He had stopped speaking, He said to Simon, "Launch out into the deep and let down your nets for a catch." But Simon answered and said to Him, "Master, we have toiled all night and caught nothing; nevertheless at Your word I will let down the net." And when they had done

this, they caught a great number of fish, and
their net was breaking. So they signaled to their
partners in the other boat to come and help
them. And they came and filled both the boats,
so that they began to sink (Luke 5:4–7).

Jesus finished His teaching, then turned
to Simon—who was a captive audience at the
time. His instructions to Simon to "launch out
into the deep and let down your nets" come
across more like an order than a suggestion. And
that command ran contrary to everything Simon
knew about fishing. In the Sea of Galilee, fishing
was done at night near the shore—not in the
daytime out in the deep. So it's understandable
that Simon would respond with an argument:
"We have toiled all night and caught nothing."
Even though he had been unsuccessful, he was
certainly an expert. For Jesus to expect such an
action after a long, frustrating night must have
seemed unreasonable. But Jesus had Simon's
boat, and now He wanted his nets—and his will.

The story is told that the Duke of Wellington, the great British commander who defeated Napoleon's forces at the Battle of Waterloo during the Hundred Days conflict in 1815, once gave a command to one of his generals, who then responded that it was an impossible command to execute. The Duke told him, "You go ahead and do it, because I don't give impossible commands." Jesus doesn't give impossible commands either—a truth Peter discovered when he finally obeyed.

This is an important step in Peter's growth. It seems as though he initially questioned Christ's command when he said, "We have toiled all night and caught nothing." But then the text says, "Nevertheless at Your word I will let down the net." He did what he was told, even though all his professional skills told him it was a royal waste of time. Notice that he called Jesus "Master." He didn't call Him "Rabbi" or "Teacher" here. He used the Greek word *epistates,* which in this context can be translated "Captain of the Boat." Peter knew who was in charge, so he responded to the word of Christ and obeyed—even though he couldn't comprehend how it would make a difference.

What was the result? Although it seemed utterly impossible, a huge number of fish were caught—at the wrong time and in the wrong way. And Peter found himself in the presence of One who could do the impossible.

One writer saw in this event a clear comparison to the apostle Paul's great doxology in Ephesians 3:20, which reads, "Now to Him who is able to do exceedingly abundantly above all that we ask or think." Peter found himself in a boat with One who was doing just that:

- Able to do—"caught a great number of fish";
- Exceedingly abundantly—"their net was breaking";
- Above all that we ask or think—

"they came and filled both the boats, so that they began to sink."

AN AWARENESS OF PERSONAL FRAILTY

When Simon Peter saw it, he fell down at Jesus' knees, saying, "Depart from me, for I am a sinful man, O Lord!" For he and all who were with him were astonished at the catch of fish which they had taken (Luke 5:8–9).

Simon's immediate response was not about all the fish he had just caught, but about the One who had accomplished it. He realized that he was in the presence of the Creator. Certainly the Christ who spoke the universe into existence had no trouble getting a few fish together to display His majesty to this poor, overwhelmed fisherman. So Peter recognized that he was in the presence of God, and he was "astonished" because what had transpired was beyond reason, description, or explanation. Only God could have done it.

Jesus revealed himself as supreme in the realm where Simon was most familiar, most skilled, and most adequate. The realization of who Jesus was elicited from Simon a most appropriate response:

Depart from me, for I am a sinful man, O Lord!

In calling Jesus "Lord," not just teacher, rabbi, or master, Simon was indicating his belief that he was face to face with deity. He saw:

- The incomprehensible difference between holy God and sinful man.
- The overwhelming burden of sin that weighs down the soul.
- The need for repentance so that his own sinful condition could be corrected.

One commentator wrote that it was as if Simon were saying, "I'm not worth it, Lord. Give up on me. I failed You when You called me before, and I will fail You again. Call someone worth Your time and trouble. Call someone You can trust. You once said that I'd be called Rock—but there's no rock in me. Give me up. I'm a sinful man."

Bishop J. C. Ryle wrote of this passage: The words of Peter exactly express the first feeling of man when he is brought into anything like close contact with God. The sight of divine greatness and holiness makes him feel strongly his own littleness and sinfulness. Like Adam after the fall, his first thought is to hide himself. Like Israel [at] Sinai, the language of his heart is, "Let not God speak with us, lest we die."

But Christ's love would not let him go. He was prepared to do whatever it took to make Simon into a rock.

AN INVITATION TO A LIFE THAT MATTERS

Jesus said to Simon, "Do not be afraid. From now on you will catch men." So when they had brought their boats to land, they forsook all and followed Him (Luke 5:10–11).

Jesus invited Simon on an adventure of faith that would radically transform his life, giving him:

A New Attitude. *"Do not be afraid."*
G. Campbell Morgan wrote, "Oh, the infinite music of it. He first said, 'Fear not.' He said it to that man, that elemental man, great emotional soul; the man who did not seem to have the strength to arrive anywhere; and He said it to him, conscious of his failure."

A New Day. *"From now on...."* It breaks with the past and changes everything. The failure of the past is replaced with a new future.

A New Purpose. *"... you will catch men."* In other words, Peter would take men alive. As God had called David and Moses to leave what they were doing to shepherd His people, He now called Simon to leave his nets and fish for people.

A New Life. *"They forsook all and followed Him."* This is an expression of radical commitment.

For Simon, everything was becoming new. Yet the extent of the transformation Jesus envisioned for Peter would not happen overnight. The man He had named "the rock" would be slow in forming.

Peter's journey had begun. He had been shaken by the power of Christ. He had felt his weakness. And he had sensed his need for One so much greater than himself. He had met the One to whom later generations would sing:

> I need Thee every hour;
> teach me Thy will;
> And Thy rich promises
> in me fulfill.
> I need Thee, O I need Thee;
> every hour I need Thee;
> O bless me now, my Savior,
> I come to Thee.

SHAKEN BY DISTRACTION

I REALLY LOVE PLAYING GOLF. It's a simple game, but it's far from easy. What makes it so challenging is that it can't be approached casually. It requires every ounce of concentration and self-discipline you have—if you're going to play well.

Golf instructors say, "Every time you swing a golf club, there are a thousand things that can go wrong and only one thing that can go right." Only by seeing and executing the correct contact of clubface and ball can you avoid an unwanted push, pull, hook, slice, or dub. Only by undistracted focus on the object of your backswing, contact, and followthrough can you put the ball where you want it to go.

It's like this in our next encounter with Simon Peter. As he slowly learned to follow Christ, he would discover what it meant to be shaken by distraction.

Matthew gave us the details in chapter 14. Jesus and His men had been engaged in a long and wearying day of ministry. As the night drew near, Christ let His disciples know that He needed some time alone.

As Jesus used the moments of solitude to commune with His Father, His men began making their way across the Sea of Galilee by boat. That's when another amazing event happened.

SEEING JESUS

In the fourth watch of the night Jesus went to them, walking on the sea. And when the

disciples saw Him walking on the sea, they were
troubled, saying, "It is a ghost!" And they cried
out for fear. But immediately Jesus spoke to
them, saying, "Be of good cheer! It is I; do not
be afraid" (Matthew 14:25–27).

The disciples were terrified by the dim, hard-
to-see appearance of someone on the water, so
they began to cry out. At the very least, they were
disturbed to see something as bizarre as this, and
they may have even feared for their own safety and
well-being.

We must remember that this would have been
an extraordinary sight for anyone to witness. But
these aren't just ordinary guys out for a boat ride.
A number of them were professional fishermen
who had spent their entire adult lives on the Sea
of Galilee. While they may have been uneducated
men, they knew water. And they knew that
people just aren't capable of walking on water.
It's not just improbable; it's impossible.

Yet Jesus called to them out of the mist

and assured them that they didn't need to be afraid. At this point, Peter acted true to form. Impulsively, he took Jesus' reassuring words not only literally but to the extreme. He let Jesus know that he wanted to experience walking on water for himself!

WALKING BY FAITH

Peter answered Him and said, "Lord, if it is You, command me to come to You on the water." So He said, "Come." And when Peter had come down out of the boat, he walked on the water to go to Jesus (Matthew 14:28–29).

Here we see the quintessential Peter—stepping out in bold, almost audacious faith in Jesus, abandoning himself to the ability of Christ. Although we have read or heard this story a thousand times, and we know that Peter is going to sink like a rock, we mustn't allow that fact to hide the amazing reality of the moment. "He walked on the water to go to Jesus." This is Peter at his best—trusting Christ absolutely and acting on that trust.

Remember, this was a professional fisherman who had spent his entire life working on the Sea of Galilee. Yet, with confidence in the ability of the Master, Peter did what no fisherman would ever be so foolish as to attempt: He climbed out of the boat and stepped across the watery surface of the Galilee toward Christ.

With Moses, God made a way through the Red Sea. With Joshua, God made a way through the flooded Jordan River. But as remarkable as those events were, this was even more so. Peter did not travel *through* the water—he walked *on* the water.

I don't think any of us would try to make a case that Peter was somehow especially gifted in water-walking or that he was somehow more spiritual than the other disciples who stayed in the boat. Far from it. In this moment of faith, Peter was walking on water because he had absolutely released himself to the Creator and His power. The power of the Creator over His creation caused Peter, the Bible's true everyman, to do one of the most supernatural things in the pages of Scripture. Peter walked on water—until he wondered whether he should be doing this in the middle of a storm.

DISTRACTED BY THE STORM

But when he saw that the wind was boisterous, he was afraid; and beginning to sink he cried out, saying, "Lord, save me!" And immediately Jesus stretched out His hand and caught him, and said to him, "O you of little faith, why did you doubt?" (Matthew 14:30–31).

Peter was suddenly shaken by the realization that he was walking on water in the midst of a storm. He became distracted and stopped looking at his Lord.

I mentioned earlier that I like playing golf.

As keeping one's eye on the ball is a fundamental of the sport, so keeping our eyes on Christ and staying focused on Him is a basic fundamental of following Him. Nothing is more important than using our Bible, our prayers, and even our fears to keep our focus on Him.

Because there are countless realities in this world that can distract us from our Lord, we need to continually make choices about whether we will allow these distractions to seduce us and draw us away from what is most important.

35

Some of the distractions we all face are

• **Fear**—the emotion we feel when we perceive that life is suddenly beyond our control instead of trusting that life is in God's control.

• **Despair**—the internal sense of loss that causes us to lose heart and hope because circumstances cloud our view of God's purposes.

• **Disappointment**—the woundedness of soul that results from placing our trust in people who fail us.

- **Stress**—the pressure that comes into our lives when we try to take on life in our own strength.

In the face of such challenges, we need to be people of purpose—people who look beyond the distractions that surround us, so that we can run the race of life by "looking unto Jesus, the author and finisher of our faith, who for the joy that was set before Him endured the cross, despising the shame, and has sat down at the right hand of the throne of God" (Hebrews 12:2).

Peter's brief encounter with water-walking was scuttled for a very human and understandable reason. He failed to focus on the Savior because he was distracted by his circumstance. His desperate, sinking cry for help, therefore, becomes a useful warning to us.

SHAKEN BY
JESUS' REBUKE

WHEN I TAUGHT for several years in a
Bible institute, I enjoyed giving tests.
I know that may sound cruel, but
testing allowed me, as the teacher, to see whether
or not all of the students were on track to
successfully complete the course and, ultimately,
to appropriately use in life the material they
had learned.

Not all tests are taken in classrooms, however.
Life often tests us with circumstances that push
or stretch us to our limits. When that happens, do

we pass the test? Or do we fall back into old habits and defeats? The pattern of having setbacks in life following progress is to be expected. It's true in our lives, and it was true in Peter's as well.

Matthew 16 gives us an especially dramatic picture of how Peter experienced a life-shaking defeat on the heels of a great moment of insight. One minute Peter was warmly affirmed by Jesus. But that affirmation was followed almost immediately by a humiliating rebuke by the Lord. In the process, Jesus' impulsive disciple helps all of us to see how quickly our emotional landscape can shift—revealing once again why it's so important for us to keep our focus on our Master.

Let's look together at the events leading up to another moment that must have shaken Peter to the core.

PETER'S MOMENT OF INSIGHT

In Matthew 16:13, Jesus had just finished yet

another confrontation with Israel's religious leaders and then traveled north with His men to the base of Mount Hermon in the region of Caesarea Philippi, a Roman outpost city that was used as a retreat for occupying Roman troops. It was here at the rocky base of the mountain that the Romans had built temples and altars to the pantheon of their Roman gods.

It seems that Jesus brought His disciples to this out-of-the-way place filled with the landmarks of false religion for one purpose— to provide the necessary backdrop for an important examination. Here Jesus would test their opinion of Him in the presence of other "options of faith." And it is here that Peter would pass the first test with flying colors—only to be thoroughly shaken by a failure he never saw coming.

A Powerful Question With Many Possible Answers. Jesus gave His disciples a test that was made up of only two questions. The first: "Who do men say that I, the Son of Man, am?" (v. 13).

41

It was like hearing the results of an ancient Gallup poll. According to His disciples, people were saying that Jesus was

• *John the Baptist.* Perhaps these people recognized Jesus' and John's shared themes of repentance and the kingdom.

• *Elijah.* Some people, having witnessed the miracles of Jesus, remembered the Old Testament stories of the powerful ministry of Elijah and assumed Jesus to be Elijah returned to the earth.

• *Jeremiah.* The people with this opinion may have seen a similarity between the ministry of the "weeping prophet" and the deep compassion of Jesus, whose care for people was bathed in many tears.

• *One of the prophets.* These people didn't want to specify but felt that Jesus demonstrated the characteristics of the great spiritual leaders of days gone by.

The disciples' summary of popular opinions

about Jesus' identity was impressive. All were favorable, yet none was adequate. They knew the crowds had been amazed by His miracles. But even those who spoke well of Jesus didn't fully grasp what they saw.

The same is still true today, 2,000 years later. When the question is asked, "Who is Jesus?" the answers come back: "A great teacher, a good man, a moral example, a religious leader." All too often, the inexpressible wonder and majesty of the real identity of Jesus is completely missed.

For that reason, it's essential that we don't miss what Jesus was doing with His disciples at the base of Mount Hermon. With the options of public opinion fresh in their mouths and with the garden of the gods of the world surrounding them, Jesus asked a second question.

A Personal Question With Only One Answer. In verse 15, Jesus took the issue of His identity out of the realm of information and made it personal. "But who do you say that

I am?" Without commenting on the different opinions of the public concerning Him, Jesus put this question to His disciples, which was His intent from the start.

Their own eternal well-being would not lie in their knowledge of public opinion or a cross-sampling of the marketplace. Their relationship with the Father in heaven would be tied directly to their knowledge of who Jesus was.

The disciples had believed in Jesus and had become His followers, but they needed to more fully understand and confess who He was before His life took a dramatic turn that would shake and confuse them. So Jesus asked His men for their own opinion: "Who do you say that I am?"

The question in the Greek is emphatic. It's as if Jesus said, "Don't parrot back the multitudes and their empty speculations. You, what do you yourselves say?" Wilbur M. Smith wrote,

Christ's miracles had two fundamental objectives: first, that of helping broken, diseased, enslaved, handicapped men and women to obtain soundness of health again, freedom from demon-enslavement, [loss of] hearing, sight, [and] the ability to walk; secondly, to glorify God in such a way that men would recognize that the One performing these miracles was indeed sent by and approved by God.

Had the disciples understood the majesty to which they had been exposed? Would their view of Christ be molded by public opinion or by the evidence? It was Peter who answered.

The Timely Answer To An Eternal Question. Peter's answer was his confession that Jesus was, in fact, the long-awaited Messiah. So he declared, "You are the Christ, the Son of the living God" (v. 16).

This is the only complete and perfect answer to the question. Every word here was clear and direct, forming a comprehensive statement of faith.

- *The Christ,* or Messiah, points out Jesus' office;
- *The Son* shows His deity;
- *Of the living God* distinguishes Him from the dead idols of paganism and points Him out as the source of all life—present, spiritual, and eternal.

Amazingly, what made the difference between Peter's confession and public opinion was not just the abundance of evidence, but the work of God in the heart to bring a life to faith. Notice Jesus' response:

Blessed are you, Simon Bar-Jonah, for flesh and blood has not revealed this to you, but My Father who is in heaven (v. 17).

The investigation, study, and weighing of evidence are not enough. It's been said that between God and man is an impenetrable curtain of unknowing. Only God can draw aside that curtain and bring to a person a certain, unshakable knowing of who Jesus Christ is. Remember, human categories will always be insufficient. This is an issue of personal discovery, and it has eternal implications.

For Peter, this was a remarkable moment. Think how far he had come in such a short time—from being a fisherman who was untrained in theology to a disciple who uttered the greatest theological statement in history. His progress had been slow, but steady. His growth had been the byproduct of his exposure to Christ. And that exposure bore fruit in a clarity of mind that was profound. Everything Jesus had done with Peter up to his moment had been to bring him to this point of understanding.

Peter's life, however, was like a roller-coaster ride with all its ups and downs. His incredible moment of God-given insight was quickly followed by a disappointing failure. Upon the heels of Peter's confession, Jesus began to unfold the eternal plan of the Father—but Peter wasn't ready for it.

PETER'S DISAPPOINTING FAILURE

*From that time Jesus began to show to His
disciples that He must go to Jerusalem, and
suffer many things from the elders and chief
priests and scribes, and be killed, and be raised
the third day (Matthew 16:21).*

The key word in this verse is *must*. This is the
divine mandate, the divine mission, and the divine
priority. There will be no looking back, no avoid-
ance of the danger. Jesus *must* go to Jerusalem,
the place where danger awaits. This intense focus
applies to the rest of the verse as well:

- He *must* suffer many things.
- He *must* be killed.
- He *must* be raised the third day.

Notice that there are two aspects to Jesus'
sense of passion:

The Human Reality. Jesus had to suffer as
the natural outcome of all that He had been
saying and doing. The people were increasingly

rejecting His message, and the religious leaders were plotting to rid themselves of Him. This was the inevitable consequence of the radical message He had presented to a spiritually deaf, dumb, and blind world.

The Divine Reality. Jesus was not simply devoted to enduring human rejection heroically. The eternal counsel of the Godhead was operating in Him, leading to suffering that would be followed by a dramatic, victorious resurrection from the dead.

49

Because Peter didn't understand this, he responded just as wrongly to this matter as he had rightly responded to Jesus' question, "Who do you say that I am?"

HIS PRESUMPTUOUS RESPONSE

Peter took [Jesus] aside and began to rebuke Him, saying, "Far be it from You, Lord; this shall not happen to You!" (v. 22).

Peter's attitude revealed a huge personal blind spot. Without realizing it, his heart was filled with presumption. In first-century Jewish culture, "Far be it from you" was a violent expression laced with anger. Simon had just confessed Jesus as the Messiah and Son of God. Yet now Peter was speaking as if he were the master and teacher of Jesus! Certainly more than he realized, he was speaking as if he understood God's will better than the Son of God whom he had just confessed.

Why? Obviously, Peter had his own plans and ideas about the future. And what Jesus had just said about suffering and dying sounded absolutely unthinkable and impossible to him.

There's a lesson here for all of us. So much of our living and thinking is rooted in our own predefined expectations. All too often, we fail to realize that God's ways are not our ways. When we don't allow God to be God, and when we don't see our dreams or goals being fulfilled, we are inclined to respond with presumption out of our own bitterness, resentment, and anger.

One commentator wrote that Peter's reaction essentially said, "This isn't what I signed up for, Lord. It was never supposed to be this way. It was supposed to be a coronation, not a crucifixion. It was supposed to be a crown of gold, not a crown of thorns. It was supposed to be a glorious throne, not an ignominious cross. This is the wrong plan. And I find it unacceptable."

51

JESUS' SHAKING REBUKE

[Jesus] turned and said to Peter, "Get behind Me, Satan! You are an offense to Me, for you are not mindful of the things of God, but the things of men" (v. 23).

In a rebuke that must have shaken Simon to the core, Jesus called him "Satan," which means adversary. Why? Because Peter was doing the same thing Satan had done in Matthew 4 when he tested Christ in the wilderness. With better intentions, but with terribly wrong presumption, he, like Satan himself, was resisting the cross for which Jesus had come into the world.

Additionally, Jesus referred to Peter as "an offense" (Gk. *skandalon*), literally, a "stumbling block." The cross was intended to be a stumbling block to the world (see 1 Corinthians 1:18; Galatians 5:11), but Simon Peter had mindlessly become a roadblock to Christ's path.

Peter's reaction shows how far he had drifted from keeping his eyes on the thoughts and purposes of his Messiah and Master.

Only a short time earlier, Peter had spoken the truth about who Christ was. But now he spoke *against* the truth—rebuking Christ and becoming a stumbling block.

I suppose Peter's words could be seen in a variety of ways, including the possibility that he was outraged at the thought of Jesus having to suffer, and he just wanted to protect Him. But

Jesus' response makes it clear that Peter's words came from a different source—a heart filled with presumptive thoughts of self-confidence and self-interest.

Such a heart is fueled by natural affection and inclination rather than by the Spirit of God. The result is that it sees only the momentary interests of "me," rather than the overarching purposes of God.

Even though none of us would knowingly choose to have such a heart, we, like Peter, can learn and experience the hard way that . . .

- a self-centered person cannot be a God-centered person.
- a self-deceived person cannot be a God-sensitive person.
- a self-driven person cannot be a God-purposed person.

It was the natural inclination of his own human nature that caused Peter to thoughtlessly assume the role of rebuking God the Son. As preposterous as that sounds, we need to realize that Peter shows us what we all are like, apart from submitting our own hearts to the will and Word of God.

Siding with Satan, as Peter did, isn't limited to the conscious pursuit of mystical, occult practice. It is the inevitable result of following personal assumptions rather than thoughtful attention to Christ.

Peter's experience of being shaken by the rebuke of Jesus gives all of us reason to consider the following questions:

• Am I submitting to the will of God in this moment—whatever it may mean?

• Am I committed to being a building block to the leading of the Spirit of God, instead of allowing my natural inclinations to be a stumbling block?

• What will motivate and compel my living? My interests or God's?

To Peter's credit, this humbling and

shattering corrective from his Lord was taken in the proper spirit. He got the message. In fact, as they moved closer to the events of the cross that Peter wanted so desperately to prevent, his commitment to remain true to Christ at all costs only intensified.

SHAKEN BY A
FAILURE TO PREPARE

THE BOY SCOUT MOTTO rings out a
timeless truth: Be prepared. Preparation
can occur in various ways. For example:

• It can be the preparation of wise decision
making that characterized American frontier
legend Davy Crockett's life motto: "Be sure
you're right; then go ahead."

• It can be the kind of preparation seen in
Proverbs 6:6-8 that is illustrated by the ant who
works hard to prepare for winter.

• It can be the preparation of an athlete who,

through sacrifice and self-discipline, prepares mentally, physically, and emotionally for a big game.

In each case, there's no substitute for preparation.

That applies to living by faith as well. We can never accomplish it in our own strength. And when we try, we fail. It's only when we are properly prepared for the challenges of life that we can face them in the grace of our heavenly Father.

The night before the cross, Jesus twice warned Peter of coming danger. But Peter ignored His warnings. The result would be another failure that would profoundly shake him forever. Let's look at the events as they're recorded in Luke 22.

JESUS' CAUTION AND CONCERN

Following the events of the Upper Room, the disciples began maneuvering for a position in what they expected to be the ruling administration of the long-awaited Messiah. After once again explaining that the leaders of His kingdom would be servants of all (Luke 22:24–30), Jesus turned to Peter and warned:

Simon, Simon! Indeed, Satan has asked for you, that he may sift you as wheat. But I have prayed for you, that your faith should not fail; and when you have returned to Me, strengthen your brethren (vv. 31–32).

Difficult moments were ahead—moments much too big for Simon. So in this first warning, Christ gave both an assurance and a means for facing those hard times:

The *assurance* was that Jesus himself would protect Peter in the testing that would follow, so that even though his heart and courage would fail, his faith would endure.

The *means* for facing those times of struggle was found in the example of Christ Himself. He had already begun His own preparation through prayer and had prayed for Simon's protection.

The second warning came when they arrived at Gethsemane. Jesus Himself was again going to prepare for the horrors of Calvary by praying to the Father (vv. 41–42). But first He told His disciples:

Pray that you may not enter into temptation (v. 40).

The message here is clear: If Christ Himself needed a time of prayer to face the difficulties ahead, how much more did the disciples need to pray! It was so important that Jesus warned them a second time:

Why do you sleep? Rise and pray, lest you enter into temptation (v. 46).

Prayer is not a security blanket for the weak of mind, nor is it the foolish chatter of people who are unable to cope with life. Time spent in the presence of the Father prepares us for challenges that will test our faith in Him—moments we could not handle in our own strength.

We see this in Peter's life primarily by

contrast. Even though Jesus urged Peter to pray in anticipation of the darkness that was coming, Peter soon fell asleep—at a critical moment. Because he was unprepared, he was shaken by another personal failure.

PETER'S COURAGEOUS STAND AND FALL

In 1 Corinthians 10:12, Paul wrote, "Therefore let him who thinks he stands take heed lest he fall." He could have been describing Peter—or any one of us who thinks that we can pass the tests of spiritual temptation by the force of our own thoughts or will.

61

In Luke 22:31, we saw that Jesus warned Peter that he was about to be tested by Satan. But he responded in typical Simon style:

Lord, I am ready to go with You, both to prison and to death (v. 33).

Jesus then told Peter that he would deny Him three times—abandoning Him in His darkest hour. Peter must have assumed that Jesus didn't know how loyal he was determined to be.

Within just a few hours, Peter showed his resolve. When Judas came with a group of armed guards to take Jesus, Peter pulled out his sword and started swinging it (vv. 47–50; cp. John 18:2–10).

Courageous as he was, Peter once again found that he needed his Teacher far more than his Teacher needed him. Jesus told Peter to put away his sword and then miraculously healed the servant whose ear Peter had lopped off with his sword (vv. 50–51; John 18:10–11).

Jesus' calm words and actions showed that Peter was out of step with the unfolding plan of God. On that night of nights, it was not physical strength that was required but a heart yielded to God's own strength and purposes. In that regard, Peter was thoroughly outmatched.

Remember, Jesus had given Peter adequate warning that a difficult time was coming—once after leaving the Upper Room and again at Gethsemane. But when Peter drew his sword, he showed a self-reliance that left him completely unprepared for what was happening.

How did this happen to Peter? Perhaps the same way it happens to us. At least two things contribute to our lack of preparation:

- We *underestimate* the nature of the situations of life that can overwhelm us in a moment of disaster and our own capacity to betray our Lord in moments of pressure.

- We *overestimate* our own ability, savvy, and strength, so that we feel no need for the provision of God's resources we so desperately require.

For Peter, this would result in circumstances and personal failure that would shake him even more than what he had already experienced.

But while acknowledging Peter's lack of preparation, let's make sure we don't miss something very noble in his resolve. When he

pulled out his sword, he was proving his willingness to go to prison or even to die for his Master.
He was trying to live up to the name Jesus had
given him. I admire his heart.

And to Peter's credit, even though the other
disciples forsook Jesus and fled after His arrest
(Matthew 26:56; Mark 14:50), Peter *tried* to
be strong. He followed the arresting mob as
they took Jesus to the house of the high priest
(Matthew 26:58; Mark 14:54; Luke 22:54).
There, however, an unsuspecting Peter would be
rocked even harder by fulfilling Jesus' prediction
of his denial.

The story of how Peter cursed and denied
that he even knew Jesus has often been told,
and the details do not require repeating here
(see Matthew 26:69–75). His fall, however, was
greater than Peter could ever have imagined.
Luke's account tells us that as the words of the
final denial were escaping Peter's lips . . .

The Lord turned and looked at Peter. Then

Peter remembered the word of the Lord, how He had said to him, "Before the rooster crows, you will deny Me three times." So Peter went out and wept bitterly (Luke 22:61–62).

Tragic. Yet it's even more tragic because it was so unnecessary. If only he had prayed. If only he had prepared. If only he had paid attention to the warnings of the Master.

This was a case in which lack of preparation led to deep regret. And we would do well to learn from Peter's mistake. Bible teacher G. Campbell Morgan wrote,

There was a time in the younger years of my ministry when I would have enjoyed fifteen minutes [flogging] Simon. But not now. I am not exonerating him from blame; but if I investigate my own heart, I am not surprised. Moreover, I have ceased criticizing him because there has dawned on me the fact that Jesus did not do so. He understood. He never gave him up.

The collapse that Peter suffered was not unusual. In fact, it is the collapse that faces all of us when we decide that we are rich, strong, and have need of nothing—like the church at Laodicea (Revelation 3:14–22). Self-sufficiency sets us up—and then tears us down. We need to fully understand:

- Paul's words: "I know that in me (that is, in my flesh) nothing good dwells" (Romans 7:18).
- Jeremiah's words: "The heart is deceitful above all things, and desperately wicked; who can know it?" (Jeremiah 17:9).
- Jesus' words: "Without Me you can do nothing" (John 15:5).

If we truly understand our own inadequacy, we will be more likely to remember Paul's words:

No temptation has overtaken you except such as is common to man; but God is faithful, who will not allow you to be tempted beyond what you are able, but with the temptation will also make the way of escape, that you may be able to bear it (1 Corinthians 10:13).

Peter failed to prepare by making use of his spiritual resources, choosing rather to depend upon himself. As a result, he experienced the collapse of a lifetime. The seismic shift that shook Peter to his core was a failure that, in human terms, didn't have to happen—had Peter trusted in the warnings of Christ more and his own resources less.

RESTORATION

P ETER IS SO MUCH LIKE US. Right up to the final hours of his three years with Jesus, he struggled with failure.

Yet that is not the end of Peter's story. As an expression of God's marvelous grace, the resurrected Christ sought out Peter and restored His dear friend to a lifetime of profitable service.

As the disciples returned to Galilee, it seems that Peter was resigned to going back to his old life as a fisherman. In a sense, he had little to show for his time with Jesus but good memories tempered by several episodes of failure.

But Jesus had something else in mind for him. He had hinted at it in Mark 16:7 when He told the women who were looking for Him at the tomb to relay a message to the disciples—naming Peter singularly—that Jesus would be meeting with them later in Galilee. If Peter perhaps thought his ministry days were behind him, he needed this reminder: Jesus had already revealed that He would visit with Peter again.

In reality, the upcoming renewal for Peter should have come as no surprise to him, for Jesus had laid the groundwork for his restoration in Luke 22:31. Even as Jesus warned Peter of his upcoming denials, He said to His disciple: "Satan has asked for you, that he may sift you as wheat. But I have prayed for you, that your faith should not fail; and when you have returned to Me, strengthen your brethren."

Changes were about to happen in Peter's life, and those changes would lead to his becoming, as

Jesus predicted to him at the beginning of their relationship, a true fisher of men (Matthew 4:19).

But before Peter returned to Galilee, something important happened. On Sunday evening of the day Jesus was resurrected, the Savior had appeared to a number of His disciples behind locked doors (John 20:19). Jesus' followers were afraid of the religious leaders, so they had gone into hiding. But that evening, the risen Lord appeared to the disciples who were there and calmed their fears by saying, "Peace be with you!" (v. 19). Also, He commissioned the disciples to continue His work, and He breathed the Holy Spirit's presence into them (vv. 21–23).

JESUS AND THE UNSUCCESSFUL FISHERMEN

After these things Jesus showed himself again to the disciples at the Sea of Tiberias, and in this way He showed Himself: Simon Peter, Thomas called the Twin, Nathanael of Cana in Galilee, the sons of Zebedee, and two others of His disciples were together. Simon Peter said to them, "I am going fishing."

They said to him, "We are going with you also."

They went out and immediately got into the boat, and that night they caught nothing. But when the morning had now come, Jesus stood on the shore; yet the disciples did not know that it was Jesus. Then Jesus said to them, "Children, have you any food?"

They answered Him, "No."

And He said to them, "Cast the net on the right side of the boat, and you will find some." So they cast, and now they were not able to draw it in because of the multitude of fish.

Therefore that disciple whom Jesus loved said to Peter, "It is the Lord!" Now when Simon Peter heard that it was the Lord, he put on his outer garment (for he had removed it), and plunged into the sea.

But the other disciples came in the little boat (for they were not far from land, but about two hundred cubits), dragging the net with fish. Then, as soon as they had come to land, they saw a fire of coals there, and fish laid on it, and bread.

Jesus said to them, "Bring some of the fish which you have just caught."

Simon Peter went up and dragged the net to land, full of large fish, one hundred and fifty-three; and although there were so many, the net was not broken.

Jesus said to them, "Come and eat breakfast." Yet none of the disciples dare ask Him, "Who are You?"–knowing that it was the Lord. Jesus then came and took the bread and gave it to them, and likewise the fish.

This is now the third time Jesus showed Himself to His disciples after He was raised from the dead (John 21:1-14).

Some time had passed after the incidents when Jesus had met with the disciples in

Jerusalem, and it appeared that Peter and his friends were not sure what their next move should be. Commissioned and empowered—yet perhaps now a bit dazed and confused—they made their way to the Galilee, where Jesus promised He would be before they got there (Matthew 26:32). While the disciples were in the Sea of Galilee region—and before they saw Jesus—some of the disciples did what many a good old boy would do when he's not sure what to do next: They went fishing.

Peter was with Thomas, Nathanael, and a few others at this time, and Peter said to them, "I'm going out to fish" (John 21:3). They jumped at the chance, and soon they were all out in the middle of the water flinging a net over the side of their boat.

Maybe the men were a bit rusty—having been away from fishing for a while—because they caught nothing. All night, they pulled their empty net from the water and cast it back in to no avail.

After sunrise, something surprising happened. A man on shore called out to them to ask if they had caught anything. When they told him of their failure, the man ordered them to throw their net on the other side of the boat.

When they did, their failure turned into a rousing success. As they pulled the net out this time, it was teeming with fish. One hundred and fifty-three large fish!

Who was this man who knew so much about fishing?

Verse 7 says that the "disciple whom Jesus loved," namely John, said to Peter, "It is the Lord!" Indeed it was Jesus Christ who turned Peter's failure on the open waters into success.

As this was taking place, Peter and his friends could have felt as if deja vu was happening all over again. The events of this fishing trip were about to mirror an earlier excursion some of these men had taken on the sea (see Luke 5). Let's look at the ways this fishing trip could have reminded them of an earlier one—one that took place just as the relationship between Jesus and Peter was beginning.

• Jesus, the itinerant preacher and healer, gave Simon Peter, the fishing expert, advice on catching fish in both incidents.

• Both times, the advice, when followed, worked better than Peter could have imagined —despite his years of experience fishing the Sea of Galilee.

• As a result of both fish stories, Peter went away dedicated to following Jesus and doing what He asked him to do.

The symbolism of this second fishing event, then, is hard to miss. But there is even more evidence that what Jesus was doing here in this early-morning session was not about fishing. It was about teaching Peter several important lessons. One major thing Peter was being shown was the contrast between his own failure and Jesus' gracious forgiveness.

Notice that after Peter, in true Simon style, jumped out of the boat and swam to the shore to meet Jesus, the risen Lord—the great servant-leader—had prepared breakfast for the men. And take special note of how He prepared this meal. There are some elements that should have stopped Peter in his tracks as reminders of Jesus' provision and Peter's own need for less dependence on self and more complete dependence on the Lord.

• *The food:* On the menu this morning? Bread and fish. Could this have been a reminder to Peter and his friends of the time before Christ's Crucifixion when He showed them that even if they had nothing to offer, Jesus would provide? After all, it's hard to forget seeing 5,000 people being fed from a lunch of five loaves and two fish. Without a word, Jesus' actions would have said, "You depended on Me before; you can still depend on Me now."

• *The fire.* And how was Jesus preparing this breakfast? Over a charcoal fire. He didn't bring the food in a bag already prepared. He didn't walk along the shore and pick up driftwood for a fire to cook it on. He used charcoal.

If we think of this incident as mostly about Peter, it is not difficult to see why Jesus went to the trouble to use charcoal for this cookfire. All we have to know is that there are only two times in the New Testament when the word translated in John 21:9 as "a fire of coals" was used. The word is *anthrakia,* and the other time it appears is in John 18:18.

Now the servants and officers who made a fire of coals stood there, for it was cold. And Peter stood with them and warmed himself.

It was while standing around the only other charcoal fire mentioned in the New Testament that Peter denied the Lord Jesus Christ. And now, with that charcoal smell wafting through the morning air, surely this memory reminded Peter of his worst moment.

And could there even be some significance

to this fact, spelled out with such clear purpose by the gospel writer: "This is now the third time Jesus showed Himself to His disciples after He was raised from the dead" (John 21:14)? Three times Peter denied his Lord; three times Jesus appeared in his presence after the resurrection.

A LESSON FOR PETER

Now, with these realizations fresh on Peter's mind, Jesus—the great Teacher—is about to patiently and carefully prepare the one he called the Rock for a life of restoration and service.

So when they had eaten breakfast, Jesus said to Simon Peter, "Simon, son of Jonah, do you love Me more than these?"

He said to Him, "Yes, Lord; You know that I love You."

He said to him, "Feed My lambs."

He said to him again a second time, "Simon, son of Jonah, do you love Me?"

He said to Him, "Yes, Lord; You know that I love You."

He said to him, "Tend My sheep."

He said to him the third time, "Simon, son of Jonah, do you love Me?" Peter was grieved because He said to him the third time, "Do you love Me?"

And he said to Him, "Lord, You know all things; You know that I love You."

Jesus said to him, "Feed My sheep" (John 21:15-17).

In this well-known interchange, Jesus asked Peter three times if he loved Him and then told him the same number of times to feed His sheep. We see again how Jesus is leading Peter from failure to success. The disciple is learning from the Teacher what his next task in His service will be: to feed the sheep, to lead the people, and to do so out of a strong love for Jesus Christ.

It seems that Jesus' graciousness and love for Peter are guiding him toward better outcomes. The one who denied Jesus not so long before is now on a course toward serving Him in remarkable new ways. The one whose poorly directed courage led him to cut off a soldier's ear is headed for a courageous and correct path of proclaiming a risen Savior.

Indeed, restoration seems ready to take hold in Peter's heart—and a whole new chapter in his story is about to be written. The one who had failed so miserably has been given new direction and new hope for success by his friend and Savior.

RESTORED
TO LEAD

THE DISCIPLES HAD at one time resigned themselves to the reality that Jesus' departure from them was the result of a Roman crucifixion. Despite Jesus' teaching, recorded in John 14, it seems that they did not understand Jesus' pre-crucifixion promises to them. From what we see of their responses after Jesus died, they must have thought that when He was placed in the tomb, they had seen Him for the last time.

Yet He surprised them all by arising from the

dead, leaving His borrowed grave, appearing to them on numerous occasions, and promising to send the Holy Spirit to guide and empower them. Only after those things were accomplished and only after the disciples had received their marching orders to "be witnesses" for Jesus in Jerusalem and throughout the world (Acts 1:8) did Jesus depart from them and ascend to heaven. Jesus made sure that their resignation had been transformed into resolve.

84

Acts 1:9 explains that after Jesus told the disciples about their mission, "He was taken up, and a cloud received Him out of their sight." Now He was gone for certain, but after Jesus' extended stay with them the disciples were different. Their mission was clear, and they seemed to have a new leader: Peter.

No longer was he leading a bunch of defeated, grieving men who feared for their lives. They had been transformed into a tiny band of witnesses who would change the world. They had been

with the resurrected Lord, and they were ready
to report for duty.

PETER'S NEW ROLE

*When the Day of Pentecost had fully come,
they were all with one accord in one place. And
suddenly there came a sound from heaven, as of a
rushing mighty wind, and it filled the whole house
where they were sitting. Then there appeared
to them divided tongues, as of fire, and one sat
upon each of them. And they were all filled with
the Holy Spirit and began to speak with other
tongues, as the Spirit gave them utterance. And
there were dwelling in Jerusalem Jews, devout
men, from every nation under heaven. . . . But
Peter, standing up with the eleven, raised his voice
and said to them, "Men of Judea and all who
dwell in Jerusalem, let this be known to you, and
heed my words" (Acts 2:1–5; 14).*

God had given Peter leadership characteristics,

but until now this disciple hadn't used them as designed.

Can we see ourselves in this man?

• We know that God has graced us with tools to use for His glory, but like Peter our fears or our lack of faith sometimes makes us sit in the background hiding our tools.

• We should also know that until we submit ourselves to the Lord and lean on His strength alone—and until we commit to doing whatever it takes to feed the sheep and use our God-given talents, we will come up as empty as Peter's nets on the Sea of Galilee before Jesus intervened.

What Peter was about to do was truly remarkable—and it can be so encouraging to us. He was about to become the first follower of Jesus to preach the gospel to the masses. The man who not long before had cowered before a young girl's comments is about to stand fearlessly before thousands and introduce a brand-new message of hope and salvation. Same man. New commitment. Unbelievable results.

We don't have a record of what went on with the disciples between the time they selected Matthias as a replacement for Judas and the time of the Day of Pentecost, but we know that they had been able to stick together as a unit. Thus, as this amazing event was about to unfold, this small group of men, along with many others, "were all together in one place" (Acts 2:1). While they were gathered, the promised Holy Spirit filled them all, which caused quite a sensation.

It is not clear exactly where this happened in Jerusalem, but it clearly was an event that drew a crowd.

According to Acts 2, the coming of the Holy Spirit was accompanied by three physical manifestations: "a sound from heaven, as of a mighty wind" (v. 2), "divided tongues, as of fire" (v. 3), and the disciples being able to "speak with other tongues" (v. 4). Although some of this happened inside a house, it got the attention of the people in the streets. Jerusalem was being visited by "devout [Jews], from every nation under heaven" (v. 5), and when they heard the sounds, they were bewildered.

Like a modern-day flash mob, the crowds gathered to see what was going on. People from everywhere assembled, and they were "amazed and perplexed" (v. 12). Controversy began to brew. The crowd grew—some understanding and accepting what was going on—and others making "fun of them" (v. 13 NIV).

The last time anyone cast that kind of aspersions Peter's way, bad things happened: he denied knowing Jesus Christ. And that was just one person. Now, however, perhaps with Jesus' words "Feed my sheep" still echoing through his mind, Peter walked right into the maelstrom. He found a place where he could address this growing, questioning, puzzled gathering—and with the eleven disciples by his side—he "raised his voice and addressed the crowd" (v. 14 NIV). But it was not just a change of heart by Peter that made the difference, and it was not just the support of his friends. Now Peter was relying on the Holy Spirit to help him be brave in the face of danger.

With Spirit-led boldness, Peter used Old Testament Scripture as his proof text and proceeded to implore these Jewish listeners to "repent, and be baptized . . . in the name of Jesus Christ for the forgiveness of sins" (v. 38 NIV).

The rock had been moved by God to kick-start the Christian church, which that day went from the 120 or so believers (Acts 1:15) to more than 3,000 followers of Jesus (Acts 2:41). The sheep were indeed fed by Peter that day—one who took on the role of leadership voluntarily and boldly.

How many times have we felt the same Holy Spirit leading that Peter responded to—yet have walked away from the opportunity? How often have we kept our tools hidden away when the Holy Spirit has prompted us to use them?

Perhaps we need to go back to the shore of Galilee and hear Jesus say, "Do you love me?" And when we answer yes, we need to hear Him reply, "Feed my sheep."

Notice that in this fascinating situation we do not see any additional promptings from God. There is no "Peter! Remember what I told you" from Jesus nor any "Go ahead, Peter. You can do this!" urgings from his friends. Peter already had been restored by His Savior, and he had his assignments. Now he was simply following through with them.

As successful as this first evangelistic message happened to be, we cannot come away from our study of this event with the idea that the restored Peter—or any of us who seek to serve Jesus—will always enjoy success. It appears that Peter was also restored to undergo adversity, as we will see.

RESTORED TO STAND STRONG

THINGS CONTINUED to go well with Peter
for a while as he and the disciples kept
feeding the sheep under the direction and
guidance of the Holy Spirit. At one point God
even enabled Peter to heal a crippled beggar
(Acts 3:7), which must have been an amazing
experience for Peter, for all who observed it, and
most of all for the beggar! Not surprisingly, this
drew a crowd, and it again gave Peter a chance
to preach the gospel, which he did fearlessly and
with a bit of an edge.

Telling the "men of Israel" (Acts 3:12) that they had "killed the Prince of life" (v. 15) and "did it in ignorance" (v. 17) may have been true and accurate, but those turned out to be fighting words for the people to whom he was talking.

STANDING STRONG IN PERSECUTION

Now as they spoke to the people, the priests, the captain of the temple, and the Sadducees came upon them, being greatly disturbed that they taught the people and preached in Jesus the resurrection of the dead. And they laid hands on them, and put them in custody until the next day, for it was already evening. . . .

And it came to pass, on the next day, that their rulers, elders, and scribes, . . . were gathered together at Jerusalem. And when they had set them in the midst, they asked, "By what power or by what name have you done this?"

Then Peter, filled with the Holy Spirit, said

to them, "*Rulers of the people and the elders
of Israel: . . . by the name of Jesus Christ of
Nazareth, whom you crucified*" (Acts 4:1–3;
5–8; 10).

Sometimes it is not possible to proclaim
the gospel without repercussions, as Peter
discovered.

Imagine the scene. A crowd is gathering
because Peter has just healed a crippled man.
His voice rings out with his powerful yet
unpopular words. You can imagine the heads
bobbing and the voices murmuring about this
fisherman's proclamations. Through the crowd
steps a contingent consisting of a priest, a group
of Sadducees, and even the temple guard.

Peter's message is cut short as he and John
are seized by the guards. They are ushered away
and thrown into jail.

Perhaps it was time to tone down the rhetoric.
Maybe it would be best to cut their losses, slink out
of town, and take the message somewhere else.

It would be easy to think this way.

But remember this: Peter had been restored by the Savior. He had been challenged to tell the story. He had been empowered by the Holy Spirit. This was no longer the sleepy Peter in the garden. This was the rock—a man with a mission. So the next day when Peter and John were hauled out of prison and asked, "By what power or by what name do you do this?" (Acts 4:7), Peter held nothing back.

He began where he had left off the day before, preaching with power and with conviction about Jesus. His message was so powerful that his listeners were left in awe. "They noticed that they had been with Jesus" (Acts 4:13). Frustrated, his accusers could do nothing more than release them and warn them to stop preaching in Jesus' name.

Peter's response tells us everything about him: "We cannot but speak the things which we have seen and heard" (4:20). Persecuted, yes.

Stopped from proclaiming Jesus? Not a chance.

It's not hard to guess what happened next with Peter. As he and the others continued to tell the people of Jerusalem about Jesus and as they continued a ministry of healing, "a multitude gathered from the surrounding cities to Jerusalem" (5:16).

Of course, the religious leaders grew jealous, and they set out again to capture Peter and the others. He continued to defy the authorities, saying, "We ought to obey God rather than men" (5:29).

Peter and others were imprisoned, warned, and then flogged for their teaching. The more they obeyed the Lord and proclaimed His word, the more suffering they endured. As we think about their situation, we must put ourselves in their shoes. We must think, *Am I willing to suffer at all for the cause of Christ?* Or instead do we tell ourselves, *I am pretty much convinced that God's responsibility is to smooth my path to heaven—free of thorns and scars and trouble?*

If that is how we feel, we could never mirror the thoughts, actions, and successes of the apostles, who "departed from the presence of the council, rejoicing that they were counted worthy to suffer shame for His name" (5:41).

And if that is the way people around the world would react when persecution comes their way, it would be difficult for the gospel to continue to be spread in some of the toughest mission fields.

Let me illustrate by telling a remarkable story that happened when I was on a teaching trip to Moscow—a time when I learned more from my students than I could ever teach them.

I made my way to the classroom one afternoon for my teaching session when I found that an unscheduled meeting was already underway. I soon discovered that a leader in the students' denomination was meeting with the students.

He was announcing to them that a bill had been introduced in their national Parliament that would attempt to outlaw the evangelical church. This action came just four years after the people had gained freedom of religion.

The leader declared to the students, "If it happens, we know what to do. We did this for seventy years under communism. We can do it again if necessary."

I was stunned by what I was hearing.

When the man left, I shared with the students my concerns and my sadness that freedoms so recently won might be so quickly lost. As a result, I asked if we could discuss what we had just heard—instead of covering the class material I had prepared.

The discussion lasted well over an hour— much of it marked by tears and fears for the future that might lay before them if this bill were to be passed. This led, quite naturally, to a long season of prayer. And then a wonderfully spontaneous rendition of "How Great Thou Art" broke out with twenty-seven Russians singing in their national tongue and one West Virginian singing in his. It was one of the most moving experiences of my life as a follower of Jesus Christ.

After I dismissed the class, a student asked to talk to me. Speaking through a translator, he said something that, these many years later, I have not forgotten. I'm sure I never will.

His name (and I'm not making this up) was Peter (*Piotr* in Russian). Here is what this modern-day disciple told me: "Thank you for loving us, and thank you for being concerned about us. But don't worry about us. We have learned that it is not enough that we live the gospel, and it is not enough that we preach the gospel. It is necessary that we *suffer* for the gospel."

In that moment, I felt that I had very little I could teach him—but my new friend Peter had much he could teach me about what it means to live for Christ and to serve Him both courageously and joyfully.

A MIRACLE ON PETER'S BEHALF

Let's examine one more incident in which Peter was persecuted because of his willingness to proclaim the gospel. Time has passed, and Peter and John have crisscrossed Israel, preaching, teaching, baptizing, and performing miracles.

The persecution had become so bad by this time that Herod the king got involved "to harass some from the church" (Acts 12:1). His hatred for this new group of Christ-followers was so intense that "he killed James the brother of John with the sword" (v. 2).

Apparently, this action pleased the religious leaders, so Herod sought to seize Peter as well. After capturing him, the king assigned four squads of soldiers to guard Peter—with the plan to bring him to trial. Things looked bleak for

Peter, as we can see in the account from Acts 12.

Peter was therefore kept in prison, but constant prayer was offered to God for him by the church. And when Herod was about to bring him out, that night Peter was sleeping, bound with two chains between two soldiers; and the guards before the door were keeping the prison. Now behold, an angel of the Lord stood by him, and a light shone in the prison; and he struck Peter on the side and raised him up, saying, "Arise quickly!" And his chains fell off his hands. Then the angel said to him, "Gird yourself and tie on your sandals"; and so he did. And he said to him, "Put on your garment and follow me." So he went out and followed him, and did not know that what was done by the angel was real, but thought he was seeing a vision. When they were past the first and the second guard posts, they came to the iron gate that leads to the city, which opened to them of its own accord; and they went out and went down one street, and immediately the angel departed from him.

And when Peter had come to himself, he said, "Now I know for certain that the Lord has sent His angel, and has delivered me from the hand of Herod and from all the expectation of the Jewish people."

So, when he had considered this, he came to the house of Mary, the mother of John whose surname was Mark, where many were gathered together praying (Acts 12:5-12).

Think about Peter's faith and how it has been strengthened and buttressed over the time since Jesus told him to "feed My sheep." He had come so far in His confidence in God that he could face certain death at Herod's hands and believe that God would deliver them—or perhaps that if he wasn't delivered it was okay.

All we need to know to recognize Peter's faith in the face of this persecution is Acts 12:6. When the danger was the greatest, Peter's confidence was so strong that he was sleeping—not in some comfy bed but in a dark prison chained between two guards. Contrast this event with the time Peter slept in the garden when Jesus needed him to be waiting, watching, and praying (see pages 60-61).

In the garden, Peter slept because he was unprepared, and his sleep brought a rebuke from Jesus. In prison, Peter could sleep because he was now prepared: equipped by the Spirit and sure that he was fulfilling God's designs for his life. One was the sleep of human complacency; the other was a sleep of divine confidence.

The principle behind it all is found in Psalm 4:8, where we read these words of David: "I will both lie down in peace, and sleep; for You alone, O Lord, make me dwell in safety."

The fact that Peter could doze in the face of danger seems as much of a miracle as what transpired next. An angel awoke Peter, loosed his chains, told him to get dressed and tie his shoes, and ushered the prisoner to freedom.

Peter then reported to the prayer meeting where his friends had been pleading for his life. In the end, it was Herod's guards, and not Peter, who were killed by the king.

LIFE IS A JOURNEY

WHILE IT IS EXCITING and informative to read of the ways Peter rebounded from his failures and became the rock Jesus created him to be, his life after Jesus' ascension was not without its moments of controversy among his brothers in Christ.

In Galatians 2, for instance, Peter and Paul got entangled in a doctrinal argument.

Now when Peter had come to Antioch, I [Paul] withstood him to his face, because he was to be blamed; for before certain men

*came from James, he would eat with the
Gentiles; but when they came, he withdrew
and separated himself, fearing those who were
of the circumcision. And the rest of the Jews
also played the hypocrite with him, so that
even Barnabas was carried away with their
hypocrisy. But when I saw that they were not
straightforward about the truth of the gospel,
I said to Peter before them all, "If you, being a
Jew, live in the manner of Gentiles and not as
the Jews, why do you compel Gentiles to live as
Jews?" (Galatians 2:11-14).*

Here Peter was rebuked by Paul for
aligning himself with men he knew to be in
error. Peter, however, would move beyond his
failings and would live out his life in service for
the living Christ.

Years later, perhaps reflecting on so many
spiritual battles fought and lost, Peter wrote:

*Be sober, be vigilant; because your
adversary the devil walks about like a roaring*

lion, seeking whom he may devour. Resist him, steadfast in the faith, knowing that the same sufferings are experienced by your brotherhood in the world" (1 Peter 5:8–9).

The lessons of Gethsemane had finally taken hold, so that Peter could use his painful life-lessons and provide us with the wisdom of 1 and 2 Peter, and in the opinion of many scholars, the stories of the gospel of Mark from his own experiences with Jesus Christ. In 2 Peter 1:1-13, it's as if Peter was reflecting on his episodes of failure by marking out a path of spiritual growth and dependence—lessons learned through pain, failure, and ultimately, a successful ministry for the Savior. And, in fact, his final words are a penned reminder of how easy it is to stumble and fall:

You therefore, beloved, since you know this beforehand, beware lest you also fall from your own steadfastness, being led away with the error of the wicked; but grow in the grace and

*knowledge of our Lord and Savior Jesus Christ.
To Him be the glory both now and forever.
Amen (2 Peter 3:17–18).*

Peter was reminding us that coming to Christ
is an event, but becoming like Jesus is a journey.
Along the way, we have ups and downs, like
Simon Peter, but we can trust in the strength of
Christ to enable us to be useful—in spite of our
human failings and inadequacies. We can grow
in Christ's grace and knowledge. And we can, in
prayer, find His mercy and grace to help us in our
own times of need (Hebrews 4:16).

Our struggle living the Christian life is a
battle that lasts a lifetime—but it's a battle
worth fighting. It will be worth it all, as the song
says, when we see Christ. For then we will fully
be like Him, when we see Him as He is (1 John
3:2)—and the battle will finally be won.